The
Law of Being

(1920)

Helen Boulnois

ISBN 0-7661-0556-3

Request our FREE CATALOG of over 1,000
Rare Esoteric Books
Unavailable Elsewhere

Freemasonry * Akashic * Alchemy * Alternative Health * Ancient Civilizations * Anthroposophy * Astral * Astrology * Astronomy * Aura * Bacon, Francis * Bible Study * Blavatsky * Boehme * Cabalah * Cartomancy * Chakras * Clairvoyance * Comparative Religions * Divination * Druids * Eastern Thought * Egyptology * Esoterism * Essenes * Etheric * Extrasensory Perception * Gnosis * Gnosticism * Golden Dawn * Great White Brotherhood * Hermetics * Kabalah * Karma * Knights Templar * Kundalini * Magic * Meditation * Mediumship * Mesmerism * Metaphysics * Mithraism * Mystery Schools * Mysticism * Mythology * Numerology * Occultism * Palmistry * Pantheism * Paracelsus * Parapsychology * Philosophy * Plotinus * Prosperity & Success * Psychokinesis * Psychology * Pyramids * Qabalah * Reincarnation * Rosicrucian * Sacred Geometry * Secret Rituals * Secret Societies * Spiritism * Symbolism * Tarot * Telepathy * Theosophy * Transcendentalism * Upanishads * Vedanta * Wisdom * Yoga * *Plus Much More!*

KESSINGER PUBLISHING, LLC
http://www.kessingerpub.com
email: books@kessingerpub.com

THE LAW OF BEING

THE LAW OF BEING

BY
HELEN BOULNOIS

LONDON
WILLIAM RIDER & SON, LTD.
8-11 PATERNOSTER ROW, E.C.
1920

CONTENTS

CHAPTER I

Man, the Seeker . . . . PAGE 7

CHAPTER II

Man, the Sentient 20

CHAPTER III

Man, the Time-server . . . 29

CHAPTER IV

Man, the Conscious 37

CHAPTER V

Man, the Ruler 46

CONTENTS

CHAPTER VI
Man in Trinity 58

CHAPTER VII
Diseases of the Spirit . . . 68

CHAPTER VIII
Hidden Mind 77

CHAPTER IX
The Kingdom of Matter . . . 86

CHAPTER X
Man, the Verb 97

CHAPTER XI
The Christ-consciousness . . . 103

THE LAW OF BEING

CHAPTER I.

MAN, THE SEEKER.

MAN has never sought more intelligently than in the present age to know something of his Creator.

No greater proof of this is needed than the increased scepticism of the hour. The hunger to know whence he came and whither he goeth is not to be assuaged by statements he cannot reconcile to his intellect and instinct. Deep, intimate, true to the very nature of his own being must be the Inevitable Law, setting him in existence. Nothing accidental, stupendous, alien, nor aloof can appeal to men accustomed to the detailed, precise, true working of (let us say) electrical mechanism. By law they work, patiently, intricately, to attain exact results. Yet, in spite of loosening powers, we cling, little creatures, to the planet, asking the old question: What are we? Is there a God?

Where shall we find some clue, some premiss, or statement that we can diligently follow to see if it can be made applicable in a wide and universal rule?

Can we trace the working of a system in ourselves that will apply equally to the working of plant, animal, and solar system? Law is undeviating. Every branch of science verifies the fact each hour. If man can find the law governing his own being, creating and sustaining himself, it is highly probable he will have sensed the power creating all things.

Let us find some statement of man's condition of being and examine it to see if it contains a principle applicable and working in wider fields. If we cannot analyse the Infinite, we can at least examine ourselves, and possibly climb from within to the without.

Even if there be a distant Personality, exterior to this planet, ruling it afar as a rajah may govern his people, yet there would necessarily follow some lines of communication, and where are we to seek traces of such communication, save in the result of the working that we can touch, analyse, and handle? The result of that working being, ourselves.

Let us make some attempt to dissect the existence we find ourselves perpetuating, and, having divided it into component parts, observe if we can find kindred power working in creature, object, planet. We must seek something in our own nature on which we can fix our eyes, and see if forces, known in our own being, can pass to wider uses or are confined and limited for ever to the little objects we momentarily know as ourselves.

Can we realize ourselves as body, mind, and Spirit?

If the last word be a stumbling-block, it may be suggested that we feel spirit as life and love; interior force, flowing irresistibly from a source yet hidden. Creatures that we are of joy and grief, none can touch the hidden spring alone making us capable of such emotion. Yet there is some quick within of whose existence we are most aware, even if dimly, when under the sway of these intensified conditions.

But our task for the moment is to choose some generally accepted premiss, such as the above, and weigh evidence not only as to its possibility in man, but in wider application.

If man exists, works, and creates in this three-fold fashion, does he do this to himself alone, or by the law of manifestation of these three principles, working, not only in him, but throughout all things in endless space and æons of time ? So that we, rooted and based in Infinite Law, are demonstrating, not merely the divine plan of a distant Creator, but the manifestation of an ever-present energy, working by a three-fold law of its own being ?

Does this Energy so impregnate man that he is, not is to be, but is body, mind, and Spirit ? Is it probable that the whole universe, all finite creation, is being worked, sustained by these three principles ? Though of the created, man alone is able to perceive the position,—to enjoy mind, and in knowing mind, to discern body and taste Spirit ?

If so, having gained this position of outlook and made the statement that man can sense his own being in these three factors or elements of existence, let us examine if this premiss seem practical in a yet wider working, applying not only to man, but to the created universe. At the same time we may see if the great world-thinkers have projected solutions of the inner working of the universe on somewhat similar lines, finding in creative energy some threefold attribute of action; not doing this blindly to accept doctrines they may inculcate, but, again, using the thinking power of which man is capable, judging from our own life and experience the value of their observations, fitting all featly together.

Throughout time men have appeared in different lands with the piercing vision of simple truth.

Through multifariousness they grasp unity. Through intermittent appearance they reach the real. Thus a doctrine arises and passes down the ages that for two reasons is called Inner or Hidden.

First, because only men with the inner vision perceive from their own hidden depths the inner or hidden meaning in the phantasmagoria surrounding them; while secondly is the necessity not only of passing on the truth to those who can perceive it, but of guarding and concealing its sacred entity from those who are not yet ready to receive it. Yet as water finds its level and interflows, so truth knows its own, and, meeting, intermingles.

Now if man finds himself to be Spirit encased by body, or body lit by Spirit, we discover the link, the communicator, the mediator between the two to be that which we for the moment roughly term *Mind*; not in any sense to define or cover its possibilities, but to differentiate this subtle force from body and Spirit.

In this *Mind* of ours we discern an invisible movement, pushing onward. Lost in unknown depths we cannot even ourselves touch and ascertain, it busies itself ceaselessly with the material world, working, in all sensible people, for improvement and advancement in conditions around us.

Among the philosophers we find Aristotle not only discerning this force, but taking it into far wider fields than man's consciousness of it. He finds for this power of push, or movement of the invisible into visible matter, another term, i.e. *form, or force.*

According to him :

Matter + form = potentiality actualized.
A sum that any man may set and work out for himself, seeing if his result agrees with that of the philosopher.

He tells us that of the two (matter and form), *form* existed first. The *Supreme Being*, Himself unmoved, is the source or mainspring of *form*. All things tend and aspire towards him by the force of *form* within, craving return to the source from which it comes ; much as a son going forth to seek his fortune keeps home as his ultimate goal. Thus *form*, travelling out

MAN, THE SEEKER 13

to the vivifying of matter, raises it by power invisible to the condition in which we now sense, not only it, but ourselves as part of it.

At once we can put the statement to the test, looking inward to see if we are *potentially actualized* by the addition or action of *form*, the movement or power of the *Supreme Being*; not a distant entity, but the ever-present source and battery of that condition of being which we are now capable of sensing. All three elements by their interfusion combining us into that life in which we find ourselves to be: Spirit, mind, and body.

In more mystical language the Zend Avesta claims the existence of this Second Power, which is the *movement* of Pure Spirit in matter, naming this inherent invisible energy, for ever working, the *Creative Word or Honover*, again with Aristotle asserting that this creative energy, this push from Divine Spirit, existed before the material universe. *The pure, the holy, the prompt Honover, I tell you clearly, O wise Zoroaster, was before the heaven, before the water, before the earth, before the herds, before the trees, before the fire, O son of Ormuzd, before pure Man, before the gods, before all the existing world.*

Even the Scriptures may fall into man's

constant error of confusing prestige with priority, yet there is persistence in this claim. We find it again in the far fragments of esoteric wisdom, introduced verbally (though possibly broken and intermixed), into the Christian Church, first by Theophilus, Bishop of Antioch, and finally in A.D. 325, by Constantine, arriving in Alexandria, summoning the Council of Nicæa and ending the conflict between Arius and Athanasius by instituting in the words that have come to us the creeds that through following years were to be known by the names of Athanasius and of Nicæa.

These echoes come from distant ages, probably rooted in the belief of the great Egyptians, who, among all seers, were those most careful to conceal their hidden meaning. Perceiving God in Trinity, this Trinity was doubtless founded on deep, scientific law of a triune existence, and—whatever mistakes may have arisen during the repetition of centuries—in the pure source of their origin profound and true meaning is embedded.

Thus the First Person of the Trinity (Supreme Being) is declared to be—*Made of none : neither created nor begotten.* The Second Person (the Creative Word) is *of the Father alone : not made, nor created, nor begotten.* And is also *the only begotten of the Father before all worlds.* While the Third Person is described as *of the Former Two, neither made, nor created, nor begotten, but proceeding.*

Our instinct finds response to these truths. Something in our most intimate selves seems to have come from longer distance than our earthly birth. This priority did not only take place (as our tendency is to make it appear) before all known things, but is going on at this very moment, if we are truly on the track and finding lines of communication with the Infinite.

Plato, realizing the gulf between intelligible Spirit and matter, between order and chaos, clearly perceives this second invisible movement of Spirit, explaining it by declaring that *Supreme Being* reserves for Himself the right of giving that movement in *essence of life,* which is to combine decaying matter and eternal life by producing *actual existence.*

Confucius also saw a moving Wisdom manifesting throughout existence, and, finding his own word to express that movement of Spirit, describes it as the *Will of Heaven.*

The Kabbala, recognizing a subtle, transmitting essence, suggests power of action, movement of Spirit, calling it *The Verb.*

In the uplifting poetry of the Bhagavad Gita, Krishna, aware of the irresistible presence of the inward Power, this push and action of invisible Spirit, pours forth:

Foolish men despise me as in human form, being ignorant that I am lord of all beings . . . on me the universe is woven as gems on a string.
. . . Imperceptibly I pervade all things.

While the Koran, rushing to the very heart and centre of all living creation, shouts aloud:

There is no God but God, the One, the Almighty.
Lord of the Heavens and of the earth, and of all that is between them.

Thus Philosophy and Religion tend to show a threefold emanation of (1) Spirit; (2) through movement or manifestation, (3) into matter.

1.	2.	3.
Spirit.	Mind.	Body.[1]
Glory.	Power.	Kingdom.
Life.	Truth.	Way.
God.	Word.	Work.
Heaven.	Thy Will be done.	Earth.

Trinity persists in recurrence. Body divides into three parts: head, trunk, and limbs.

[1] The table should also be verified by being read downwards.

Mind busies itself in us as memory, observation, reasoning. Indwelling Spirit becomes perceptible to men as life, love, and truth. Always the existence of each of the three depends on intermingling its powers with the other two. None has a separate and independent entity, existing to itself as a thing apart. Thus there are not three lives, a life related only to truth, a life related only to life, a life related only to love; but One life. *So also there are not three Spirits, but One Spirit.*

1. The Glory = The Substance. The One and Absolute Being. I AM.
2. The Power = Emanation of Intelligence. The movement of grace. THAT I AM.
3. The Kingdom = The action of all set going. The Presence of God in the midst of His creatures. I AM THAT I AM.

Feebly these tables try to represent:
(1) The Omnipotent Presence of Spirit. (3) The Material put in active use. (2) The link between them, the going-forthness of Spirit in intelligence, movement, and life, somewhat like the rays of a sun, though, instead of falling upon, this force pierces, impregnates, and vivifies through creation.

Yet another simile, again drawn from the material world, is that of a tree. The leaves of a tree are not only fed by sap, but the essential, though invisible part of the leaf, is sap. On this withdrawing, the matter of which the visible leaf is composed perishes.

Again, the sense of a spoken word, passing from one to another, remains intact in the speaker, while illumining the understanding of the hearers. So, too, the light from a torch can communicate light to others, remaining undiminished in the giving: thus does Glory pass with Power into the Kingdom, sustaining no loss.

An outside God could not remake this world without first destroying it. He would not be the Immanent Cause of being, but only a sovereign architect. Yet creating, God Himself must wait for creation to awaken to His Presence.

To man alone, endowed with consciousness, is reserved upon the planet the delight of realizing himself in the threefold existence of body, mind, and Spirit; but at once he must concede that the mind in himself (or rather, his conscious perception of it) can only represent a feeble portion or reflexion of the Creative Intelligent Energy, passing from pure

Spirit into every part of his body, holding it now in life and health by an understanding control. Even in his own body intelligent force is working, directing, upon which his very existence depends, but as to which his mind remains a blank. He must realize a wider working in his own body of the force Mind than that of which his brain is immediately conscious, if he is to sense in his own being the movement sustaining the Universe.

CHAPTER II.

MAN, THE SENTIENT.

DOWNWARD must go man's face in struggle for survival. Though breath of the Living God, he finds himself encased in dust of the earth. To the earth he must look for his sustenance and that of his dear ones. Anxiety for those dependent on him weighs his thought with belief in the necessity and durability of matter.

Like the Sphinx bound to a plough with folded wings, his eternal self must submit to an earthly yoke. A dual state of existence in which two elements, body and Spirit, each foreign to other, are bridged by invisible mind, man finds himself, intelligible Spirit, at war with chaotic matter. His body feels, touches, and knows the one side of nature, putting him into being; the other side is invisible, untouchable, to certain characters almost unthinkable.

If these three elements or laws of being are co-existent, co-equal, not one without the other, but by a mingling of all three, each making the necessary expression of present existence, culminating in man, he finds himself in a universal fight or combat to hold what Confucius calls *the just mean* between them. His task is, not to deny or mitigate the existence of any, but by fine balance of all three to aid and abet every part, to master and dominate in due relation each to the other, adjusting them to accompanying environment.

The passing of Spirit — through matter — makes the cross +, the web and woof of man's immediate condition of being.

Drawn to this planet by attraction for existence, the Spirit, encrusting or clothing itself in matter, divides into millions of fractional sparks. Thus the Son suffers in each, seeks, fights in Himself, has not where to lay His head; for hidden in the depths of His desire lies the germ of Living Spirit, penetrating, piercing the core of his existence with incessant onward urge and push.

Do. Act. Be. This Secondary Power, the movement of Pure Spirit, cries within him without cease. And if man be deaf and blind to this inward call, matter is raised as a bludgeon to beat him into action.

Around us in plant and rock this Spirit of

22   THE LAW OF BEING

Life is seeking other and beautiful expression, more tranquil because unconscious.

In insect and animal we perceive an unconscious exercise of intelligence, a flow of love, no less intense because it cannot look round upon and measure itself. In the lower order of existence we observe implicit obedience to instinct. In the higher, we recognize reasoning power and spiritual nature.

Unlike plant and insect, man cannot address himself to any task without an internal questioning, caused by the conscious working of mind within him. Not only is he compelled to question the immediate expediency of all his ways, but an accompanying sense of right and wrong, probably but little known to the lesser creation, is present within him with the earliest stirrings of this consciousness. Within himself he finds a stern critic of his acts.

> *Nor in thy folly say, I am alone!*
> *For seated on thy heart, as on a throne,*
> *The Ancient Judge and Witness liveth still.*

In no sense and at no moment can he exist merely as a body without the consent, even to the smallest of his actions, of his mind. He cannot close his consciousness to any three of the elements of which he is made.

To what end should man thus be chosen to be the sentient tool of matter, mind, and Spirit?

Why do these three, meeting in man, so mingle as to render him alone on this planet capable of constructive thought, of power of reasoning, imagination, and memory? Combining in man, they contrive to make—what? A mechanical toy? Or a powerful working engine?

The answer lies in the fact of an outside or an inside Creator.

Are these forces projecting power in transitory fashion, like sparks from a furnace, to make objects at which they can look? Or are they, by the very law of existence, compelled to impregnate each other's substance, thus finding expression in each other and causing the projection of visible objects, before they can consciously exist?

If the latter is the case we are not merely the sport and prey of alien powers, but the living expression, the best conveyance yet possible on this planet, of their own energy and substance that Spirit, Mind, and Matter, desiring to be sentient each by means of the other, can push forth; not creating and abandoning, but positively being us, ourselves.

THE LAW OF BEING

Yet to admit this, it might be complained, would be to sink our identity. But if we can lose our life even momentarily in the presence of these Everlasting Forces, better still, if we can identify the self of the moment with these Eternal Powers, we spring into larger spaces to live wider lives, drawing force from inexhaustible stores.

Follows the question: if, then, we are the expression of the one great life-force, one great Spirit, why this haunting sense of separation? If we are not in reality and truth myriads of segregated existences, why each *I* apart and alone? As each most certainly is. Not father, wife, lover, nor brother can quite reach the essential spot of man's ultimate loneliness.

We must return to the seek of Spirit into matter.

Still Spirit, gross matter cannot realize consciousness until, mingling each in the other, some prick can be given, some quick be touched, causing the uniting two to recognize each other.

And how is such quick to be touched? How can the prick be given?

Edward Carpenter replies: *It was only by pinning sensitiveness down to a point in space and time by means of a body; and limiting its perceptions by means of bodily end-organs, that these new values could be added to creation—the local self and the sense of identity.*

Sense of personal identity, probably unknown to bird, beast, and plant, finds life expression in man. Sense of self, the all-important ego, causes sensations in man, possibly peculiar to himself alone. He becomes to himself a centre round which all else revolves. With certain power of creation is also passed into his being sense of responsibility in the acute and personal capabilities of his own identity.

So that the very urge of the Living Spirit, rather than assuring him that, so far from being to himself alone, he is but a bubble on the stream of one universal life, only intensifies his loneliness, leaving him in his highest moments but one parent—the Invisible.

We need not ask—to what end this high sense of responsibility and loneliness in each separated individual ? We need but look on the achievements of the race, built upon individual and personal effort. Nor could there be many found, if indeed any, who would seek to part with this privilege, even if a price must be paid. Not only does man's outward world yield to the pressure of this, his inward urge ;

but far within his own quiet depth, Spirit, growing conscious in matter, enables him to sense his source.

Following the conception of Spirit seeking manifestation in matter, let us see if it can give further food for thought in the puzzle of existence, if we bring its searchlight to bear upon the problem of sex.

In mystical language, ancient Scriptures proclaim truths we may not have eyes to read nor patience to dissect.

God created man in His own image—in the image of God created He him; male and female created He them.[1]

We pause to ask why *him*, but later *them* ?

A certain type of formalist, believing in an outside Creator, seeing man as His toy, a puppet looking like Him, examining his own physical side of life, imagines that God, making man out of matter with end-organs, probably similar to His own, next creates a sort of other creation—woman, to fill his physical wants.

Not so.

Let us perceive the Infinite, manifesting in finite, meeting the difficulty of making Matter realize the presence of indwelling Spirit. Some

[1] Genesis.

movement, desire, aim, must be planted. Some lack that will set up stirring and striving in dumb matter.

Instead of making man—one, they are made two : *male and female created He them.*

In both separated parts are thus implanted longing—the first conscious movement of Spirit in matter. In union, joy is caused ; a breath of the Living Spirit manifest. Had man and woman been one,[1] in inert self-satisfaction, this emotion (or motion of invisible Spirit) could not be experienced.

Yet the eternal feminine and the eternal masculine — Motherhood and Fatherhood — doubtless existed prior to man's appearance on this planet, being set indeed in the very inner essence of Supreme Being. These, the qualities of His own Being, He passed into the creatures of this planet, that with pride and joy, protection and sorrow they might indeed share His very nature and being, passing through themselves the abundant love He pours upon His children.

Thus are they made to partake of His image and likeness. Thus Intelligible Spirit causes sensation in irresponsible matter, sensation

[1] The Scarabæus proper is of one sex. See James Duncan on *Entomology*.

varying with the spiritual or animal tendency of those in whom it is aroused.

Yet however dense may be the body in which Spirit is struggling to consciousness, in joy and sorrow, finite calls to the Infinite.[1] Multifariousness yearns to unity. Pure Intelligence operates through matter, and Pure Spirit exercises supervision, not upon, but within, the creature; out of the lesser calling to the larger. Creating and filling need, not that man may be satisfied with less, but that the quick, touched within him, springing to higher longing and aspiration, may finally attain, through the prevailing quality of the highest part of his own nature—Spirit.

[1] " But woe being come, that soul is dumb
  That crieth not on God."—E. B. BROWNING.

CHAPTER III.

MAN, THE TIME-SERVER.

The mighty atom has ceased to exist. Scientific men all the world over have destroyed the theory of inertia, of a solid, immovable base, even in an atom.

Matter consists of perpetual movement, of vibration, too vivid to be perceptible to the human eye. Its very existence depends on change—on destruction and construction continually replacing each other. Magnetic force drives, that which appears to us still, into movement too swift and minute to be perceptible to us.

Generally as we imagine matter, mind, and Spirit, we mentally see the spark of life, fire that cannot cease from action, passing perpetually into matter, which lies inert, waiting to be penetrated by the movement of Spirit, the Verb, the River of life, generating power as it emerges from Divine Wisdom. The mother, numb matter, stirred to action, brings forth her child with joy and pain.

30 THE LAW OF BEING

So immediate and incessant is this quickening that matter is never heavy, numb, inert, however it may appear to us.

Incessant are its vibrations, endless its movement. Living protoplasm never ceases to resolve into differing constituents. Within the body, corpuscles decay, perish, and are born anew; the very health of the whole depending upon the speed and precision with which this is accomplished. Thus from the dead rise the living. An inward resurrection of the body perpetually continues. The very element of matter, in fact, is not solidity, but endless change. The Spirit of Life holds unity, cohesion, some oneness of purpose in each body, built up of myriads of vibrating ions and corpuscles, changing endlessly with a speed that becomes visible to our eyes when the Sublime Energy, withdrawing at death, abandons matter—whose swift vibrations are then seen crumbling and decaying from the instant the unifying force is not in them. This same decay with the addition of re-birth is the action of matter, even when to our eyes it appears most solid and compact.

There is no being, only becoming.[1]

Bergson might be quoted in this particular.

[1] Buddhist text.

We can also return through the ages to the wisdom of the Kabbala; to learn that *Nothing is born, nothing perishes absolutely. Things only lose their ancient place.*

This theory that existence, as we know it, is made up of vibrations, atomic conditions, incessantly changing and moving, putting on a different appearance, makes Time a necessity, almost a reality, to this phase of existence. While we change, we must have time to do it. Change and succession of their own nature create a measuring: *So long from this. Next follows that.* The very action of being thus creates the sense of measurement that men call Time.

As we are in matter, so also we are in time. *That which changeth not* alone needs not time, is not of time.

Those who speak in light manner of a realization of the Nothingness of Time and Matter may pretty surely never have sensed it; for the very substance through whose vibrations we alone exist on this planet is matter, while every ion and corpuscle of it in the vibration alone holding it in existence constitutes time. Thus our state of being is punctuated with time, and even our minds work not all at once, but in succession.

Hume has long since warned us how constantly we mistake, in looking about us, this abiding sense of succession for such realities as cause and effect. We suppose, for example, that one and two actually make the next object three. That we call this *one* and that *three* is only a method of dealing with the limitations of our minds. In themselves they are neither *one* nor *three*.

If a man would stand free from this confusion, he has only to call to the Infinite within him. Though a unit among millions of like units, he cannot sense himself as a number, waiting his turn, to the great Source and Father of all. As Spirit calls to Spirit this sense of numbers is lost. Momentarily we may touch the great Oneness in stillness impregnating all. Time ceases. We have not to wait our turn, nor the conclusion of one vibration making place for another. We have passed from finite to Infinite. And we know it is the real; for difficult as it is to us to think of ourselves, or of any of the myriad objects with which we find ourselves surrounded, as existing without time or space, it is perfectly impossible to conceive time and space as self-existing entities, entirely unrelated to objects.

The daily invention and regularity of time are

rendered necessary to us by the unending order and regularity with which our vibrations vibrate.

For the most ordinary example of this we need only regard the process of digestion between meal and meal; the regularity with which the perishing and new-born protoplasm within us calls for fresh alimentation. Dinner-time is probably the best-known time in all the universe, making audible call to animals as well as men. It recurs with a regularity which may well make its persistency pass for us into fact, and so long as material existence can only continue while attention is paid to this measurement, most of us will doubtless regard this present necessity of existence as solid reality.

Far more strange is it that a brain, necessarily working through the vibrating, changing nature of its material substance in perpetual succession of *next-each-otherness, so long from this, so far from now*,[1] a brain that cannot even heap thought upon thought, but must take each separately, each in order of time, each in succession, is capable of sensing some part of itself unrelated to time. Some condi-

[1] These terms are borrowed from A. D. Lindsey on *Immanuel Kant*.

tion of the higher order, Spirit must also form part of man's own being. Otherwise the gulf would be unbridgable, irremediable.

Though man must perceive in succession, he has in himself, unrelated to time and space, the quality by which he is able to set out to perceive. Again, though restricted by the sense of *So far from here—So long from this*, restricted by the very nature of his body, existing solely in these conditions, certain intuitions remain with him, unrelated to measurement. Of such is the sense of right and wrong. Time has nothing to do with them. Some namelessness in himself arises and shouts as from eternity an inborn and everlasting Yes or No.

Again, there is no one who has a great gift, who calculates, analyses rapidly, has a talent for words or languages, who is not aware of a power almost foreign to himself in his brain. He knows these things. He does not have the trouble to get to know them, to make himself know how to know. From a source in himself this knowledge springs. A source that is disconnected with the monotony of routine, of measurement of time bound up in the getting to know, that he may possibly observe in his neighbour.

Then, too, the source of the affections lies far deeper than the vibration of measurement. The busy little thinking self may forbid one to love or hate. Irresistibly from unknown depths surges the tide, throwing down barriers of calculation, sweeping over boundaries to reign in our beings with primeval force, flinging away time, succession, and measurement of matter.

Nor should we be justified in stating that while matter vibrates, Spirit is still. Spirit may possibly be yet swifter vibration. Our task for the moment is to sense an essential difference in their vibrations: to know that the vibration of matter is an affair in time, of that non-existing quality for which a name must be found, because it is the measurement made necessary by the law of successive change, of perpetual alteration of matter, which, as it alters, must have time to do it. One point must be clearly made: While time is a necessity of existence to changing matter, it is of non-existence to Supreme Being, whose action is spontaneous, simultaneous. It is man's limited, material brain that requires time for his mind to review, marshal, and observe. *That Which Is* senses all simultaneously.

Of the essential nature of Spirit, whether yet swifter vibration, whether stillness, we are not competent to declare. Scriptures may be touching eternal verity when speaking of the Rest of God.

When seeking within communion with the Most High, it is in peace and stillness we best approach the great Spirit, the hidden, inner Life, Source of all this feverish energy; while timeless truth assures us that *in quietness and confidence* still lies *our strength*.

CHAPTER IV.

MAN, THE CONSCIOUS.

COMMON-SENSE and intelligence permeate all existence.

Notably do we observe this in the actions of insects and animals. Not only does every cell, corpuscle, nucleus of protoplasm, forming and reforming them, work with ceaseless, active usefulness, but this same activity, passing without break through the completed body, urges them to sensible action in much the same automatic or unconscious fashion.

It is a very act of nature to the ant to fall into rank and accomplish its own special task in the community of which it finds itself a member. Yet closer to our view is our benefactor the bee; the perfection of whose hives, the routine of whose daily work would certainly be of a more fluctuating character were each bee in a position to direct its own individual operations. Mechanically the little creatures obey the law of their natures; ruling and interfering with them no more than we could interfere with our own interior laws of germination and birth, which take part automatically and with undeviating regularity.

The process of cell construction, honey gathering, wonderfully bound up with the hourly necessity of their existence, passes into sensible activity in the bee without his will or wish, or the participation of his imagination. In the same way we observe the inner urge in birds, again closely related to their physical being, not only telling them to mate in spring, but the high intelligence passing through them induces them first to provide nests from twigs in tree-tops, homes for themselves and nurseries for their young, passing to yet further activities in the migrating birds, sending them safely from continent to continent, delivering lands from insects that without them might be a pest.

In all this life and intelligent movement we mark again the three-fold law of being. Swift vibrations of matter form the body. Persistent action of Spirit, possessing the dumb material, not only endows with life, but with the movement of common-sense activities.

Yet mind lies hidden to the consciousness of its busy little transmitter, which we can more

MAN, THE CONSCIOUS

easily conceive as in some sense conscious of the Great Source of Life in its being, Spirit Itself, the Father of all.

Interesting as discussion on this latter point may be, and not without forcible argument, for joy must be with the birds, the conscious breath of Living Spirit, it is on the working of mind we would concentrate attention, particularly on such working of it as may now be familiar to the human race.

Note the now : for the next somewhat bold question is to suggest that man, in the process of evolution, is slowly evolving more consciousness of mind. An evolution that he must, after a certain point, push forward or retard himself. Powers lie hidden in the material manifestation called man ; laws of being, of which he is capable, still untested and untasted by him.

We certainly see around us differing states of consciousness of mind, both in ourselves and our neighbours ; and, while we keep in perspective this liquid, interflowing transfusion of thought, dull in one, brilliant in another, penetrating and perspicacious in a third, showing in flashes here, but in steady transmission there, shining through the curious intermingling of qualities, such as courage, patience, laziness, not without their influence upon it, we may well perceive this mind to be in a transitional stage, and may even consider whether some shutter were once closed upon this thinking power in man; so that he, too, at a different epoch of existence lived like insects and animals—unconsciously.

A great gap lies between man and the animal world. Even if certain animals think—man does more, he thinks that he thinks. He can watch his own thinking power in action. He is conscious of it.

And if we look to yet widening consciousness we must not confuse it solely with progress due to the accumulated industry of the race. We inherit the tangible efforts of our forefathers; but this is not to say our inventive efforts, point of view, or consciousness are larger because we start from a bigger material basis. It is not to additions we blindly inherit we must turn our eyes, but to the increased working of the individual mind, developing in our own interior.

Now it is curious to note that the old-world allegory of Adam and Eve, enthralling attention with truth, for every man and woman know themselves to be those simple, primitive beings, living in peace and joy in the garden among the beasts, might be the history or por-

MAN, THE CONSCIOUS

trait of man at the moment when he breaks from obedient instinct into conscious thought. It is curiously exact as to sensations likely to occur.

Two objections may be put forward to this supposition. First, that this consciousness was not likely to burst upon anyone all at once, doubtless being very slowly evolved. Secondly, that it would be happening to all human creation and not to a specific man and woman.

But teachers take single characters at their most dramatic instant to figure forth, not merely those characters, but the essential man and woman hidden in the depth of all.

No one would gainsay that Adam stands as prototype, figure-head, father, original man. The same might be said of woman and Eve, had not unfortunately a certain slyness been mixed with the character. Though the going-forwardness she exhibits in contrast to Adam's more sluggish temperament most would agree to be fundamental in her sex.

These, however, are side issues. Let us seek plainly into the tale, applying the searchlight of the idea that it describes man's transition from blind instinct to conscious thought.

Let us picture primitive man and woman,

no more aware of themselves, no more capable of consecutive thought or measurement of action than are the animals, existing from moment to moment, obeying the insistent dictates of nature within; eating, drinking, sleeping, wandering. Probably on happy, friendly terms with animals about them, neither fear in themselves, nor the carnivorous smell of flesh-eaters, exciting fear, dislike, or appetite of the beasts. Life so easy, without wear, tear, hard work, responsibility, that fresh air, sleep, water, and slight alimentation would suffice all wants. No movement of brain or mind. Sharp, physical sensations alone susceptible. Love and hate would be in them, unnurtured, also undimmed by recollection and imagination, primeval in quality. Yet even when swayed by intense affection, man would blindly BE, without the power of turning upon himself to dissect, regard, and observe.

Given the moment when some subtle force, creeping through the brain like a serpent, awakens it to fuller activities [1]; given the

[1] In Eastern religions the serpent recurs as a symbol, usually as an attribute of the Second Power, often as Wisdom. Tail in mouth completing the circle, the Serpent symbolizes Immortal Life. If life, then health. Moses raised the Serpent in the Wilderness. It is still worn by army surgeons.

tasting and testing of some larger power from knowledge, which, like a tree within, imperceptibly grows, throwing out branches; let a branch of this knowledge touch some inner quick, quicken some hidden spring. Like a kitten opening its eyes, man sees, becomes aware, and—mysteriously awful process, not yet understood—thinks.

Then do troubles cluster thickly upon him. Self-consciousness plunges him into criticism. Strange fears, shames seize upon him. He looks upon his mate, and, feeling his own difference, shrinks from her eye. An intense desire to hide overtakes him—to conceal not only his naked limbs, but his thoughts.

Strange, wise old Book! Do you note how it tells that having eaten of the Tree of Knowledge, man may also eat of the Tree of Life and become as the gods? Is this Branch also growing up within us?

But, for the moment bewildered, blinded by new cares, responsibilities, anxieties, scourged with the fear of the morrow, man goes forth to fresh combat, raising his own enemies, in himself, in the beasts he now dreads and slays, in his neighbours, against whom he pits his hand, fighting darkly, blindly for himself and his dear ones. And yet . . . enjoying the fight! Putting forth powers, as yet untasted, reaching into depths and heights of his manhood.

The high Angel-power in himself pushes him forth to make use of his new forces. With flaming sword it drives him on to endeavour, barring the way to content that would end in sluggish inertia. He has touched Divine Urge, and deep in the heart of his nature must hear its insistent call. Creative energy is loosed in him.

And if the Angel-power is in himself, the Devil-power is likewise there. Lucifer has fallen. Light of Eternal Comprehension is now flickering feebly in the too narrow space of man's existence. The Light that lighteth the world is darkened by the compression of his small dimensions. Not yet can the ray burst through him as it should, not dimmed, but glorified. Not yet, not until he has made his ultimate choice between good and evil, blessing and cursing, life and death; and, grasping life, comes into his full inheritance.

And woman? If with consciousness toil has fallen upon Adam, into her hands are given the safe keeping of the honour of the race. She is to crush down *Desire*, risen to a menace against her children.

MAN, THE CONSCIOUS

No longer does man blindly yet sensibly obey the call of nature. He looks upon his acts and multiplies them at volition. The gift of procreation, now under his caprice, may be turned from health to disease.

Woman is guardian. She is—temptress or Mother. Doubtless the further Branch of the Tree of Life cannot blossom and bring forth fruit until she fully acquits her charge; while with the sweat of his brow Adam's toil increases.

CHAPTER V.

MAN, THE RULER.

Is man master of his fate? Is he driven as leaf upon breeze?

Interior powers confuse him. Not only exterior conditions multiply upon him, unknown, difficult to foresee; but forces, far within himself, constantly drive, surprise, and compel him.

If creation on this planet be composed of interacting matter, mind and Spirit, man alone is the conscious instrument or possessor of mind. This active power of push, this movement of Living Spirit into matter, can be known in his own intimate being solely by him.

He is thus placed in a unique position. No longer the blind instrument, if he chooses to master his own powers by allying them consciously with the higher laws of being, he is raised to an active partnership with this

Second Power of the Universe. He himself in his own person is called to be the conscious Verb, the Word made Flesh, while Creative Spirit dwells in his midst.

Doubtless this must be the end to which we are made; but many among us still wander in the Wilderness of our own desires, caprices, emotions, entangled by the maze of ourselves, unable to reach the Promised Land, of which the depths of our being most constantly assure us.

Yet man, as the one mind made conscious on this planet, can at least examine the invisible ingredients of which he is made.

Let us then turn within and analyse our own constituents by the use of the strange capacity of conscious thought.

Into the brain itself pour emotions, affections, qualities, unrelated to pure thought, yet perpetually bearing influence upon it. Let us use the brain in a quiet moment to dissect and separate these influences, arranging them, as a good chemist may analyse.

All men are created of the same material. Each differs from other by the intermixture of this material, by the altering quantity and interplay of the same fundamentals. Let us tear these natural, internal functions apart from each other. Name them. Mentally prevent their intermingling while examining them. By some such method, clearing paths through the tangle, we may assist dominion over our own inward realm.

By the power of mind in man he can detect in himself:

1. Conscious thought.
2. Qualities. (Courage, Idleness, Kindliness, etc.)
3. Emotions. (Love, Admiration, Grief, etc.)
4. Sense of right and wrong.
5. Will.
6. Sensations of the body; including messages from the five senses.

Let us place in a category apart the power of *thought*. Man thinks. He is capable of ranging memories and collecting creative ideas. He can correct his actions, glean from experience, forecast and image future events. By the immediate use of this power of thought we now purpose to review other inner faculties.

The next things against which we knock are qualities.

Interplaying with quiet, calculating reason we discover the quickening of other impulses, unconnected with the brain, though perpetually colouring it. Not outside circumstances, but wayward children of his own inner nature are compelling factors, making man the mere prey of the unexpected, far within himself. *Qualities* are inextricably woven into the very texture of his existence.

Of these, each one owes something to heredity, physical condition, environment, education, and example; yet when carefully sifted will be found primarily to have intrinsic entity, or power, in themselves to be the raw material out of which each man's character is built.

One thing is certain : no man has originally thought these qualities into existence. However great his subsequent power of altering and modifying, he finds them implanted within him. Seeds, already sown, spring into active existence, creative or destructive in tendency, before he is even aware of their presence, sometimes first made known to him by his own acts.

Let us then, like a general surveying troops, marshal these forces within us, observing both capabilities and disqualifications, and above all the position that should judiciously be accorded to each.

Courage, Patience, Fear, Temperance, Caution, Magnitude, Generosity, Malevolence, Spite, Envy, Conceit, Pride, Enthusiasm, Gratitude, Benevolence, Temper, Aptitude, Humour, Sarcasm, Selfishness, Altruism, and others.

Each in turn should be subjected to examination as to the proportion due to heredity, environment, education, physical condition, and finally reduced to the naked or intrinsic personal power of the quality itself.

The extraordinary faculty of being straight with himself is the gift of every man, does he but choose to exert it and not deliberately choke it. This act of examination, of inward arraignment, makes man momentarily the possessor and puts him for the instant in conscious dominion over his qualities. Does he choose, he can go further and strip them of power to drive him as leaf before the wind.

Although bound into his very being, although *a priori* in origin, man can strengthen or weaken these forces at will. Admiration inculcates growth as surely as water will assist a bed of young plants. Let a man truly admire [1]

[1] Note in admiration the invisible quickening power of Spirit. Apply in larger sense to the working of Mind creating all. *He that hath ears to hear, let him hear.*

MAN, THE RULER 51

a quality, even in another, insensibly he strengthens it in himself; while loathing will assist it to dwindle away. Let him observe occasions on which some quality in himself—possibly partly inherited—that is increased in value by the nurture of a forefather, lifts him through some difficult situation, and, in giving praise to the Inward Power, putting him in possession of this force, he increases it. Let him detect occasions on which he has been the prey of some undesired quality, such as spite, and in the inward laceration he will give himself, the quality sickens and decays, receiving mortal blows. The danger is in the blind fool who coddles weakening qualities, calling them by prettier names.

Next in our search for natural functions we may touch Emotion. Forces unrelated to the power of conscious thought, by the use of which, however, man is privileged to sense, measure, and weigh them. Emotions, though doubtless fostered by circumstances, helped or hindered by qualities, spring hot from so deep a source that man is conscious of their eternal origin, knowing them greater, more everlasting than the little mortal creature in which he now finds himself encased.

With the uprush of this Spiritual Power

from the very deep, his thinking mind may be overwhelmed as by a torrent, leaving the essential self the victim of unknown forces within him. Now is the moment that his qualities, if untamed, may rush in and destroy him, or on the contrary as trained troops come instinctively to his aid.

Love can be man's closest tie with the Infinite. Gates within him open wide to larger spaces. Instinctively he knows himself the channel of immortal force. Greater than himself is the power pouring through him. Here in his proper person can he taste the Second Creative Power, the Verb of God, using him to pour protection, tenderness, happiness to other of His children, and in thus using, strengthening, lifting, propelling him to higher aims and larger life.

He can sense the clean, unspotted Spirit of love in his midst, using his mind to tear from it pride, self, appetite, and contaminating influence.

Admiration, offspring of love, (yet so closely related to thought that we might imagine both to be its parents, for intelligence must consent to love before admiration can come into being,) spring, too, from source so unfathomable and infinite that man, while he can influence, can never create them in himself.

Sorrow, joy, and grief, as we see by their being created in one by conditions utterly inadequate to arouse emotion in another, are actual spiritual entities in themselves. These, too, may toss our inner selves as leaves in a tempest. Yet these mesmerizing powers have no control over habitually governed qualities, which lift to the ennobling of the self the lash that may be driving it, bringing safely through tempest to sweeter, higher calm.

Strangest perhaps of intrinsic powers is the natural function of the sense of right and wrong. Education may make use, even selfish and wicked use, of this instinctive sensation, so that a child may be inveigled into false application of the principle. He may be taught that wrong is right, and right is wrong, and be blinded into false use of the instinct; yet the shrink, or the intuitive spur to will, given by this rooted belief springs from depth within, unfathomable by man.

That this inward faculty becomes evident with the awakening or widening of consciousness is shown by the fact that the dog, his life complicated by continual intercourse with man, acquires, probably from his influence, knowledge of this latent faculty in himself. A dog can be taught not to touch his dinner till a given signal. Strange presence of guilt within, of an accusing, judging self, will manifest in his appearance if he trespass against the rule. Here is a quality no man could put into a dog, nor for that matter into himself. He can rouse his knowledge of it, make use of it; he may even turn it to ill purpose and abuse it, but such strong forces as calculation or emotion cannot remove more than momentarily its presence from his midst; for, inextricably interwoven with sense of wrong are the functions of guilt and fear. Some inward sensation of shattering accompanies the first step of ill-doing, quite apart from outward dread of discovery.

Nothing separates Mind from the sense of its source, Spirit, so surely as evil. A blunting of finer perceptions—the beginning of death—like paralysis, creeps all unaware upon the ill-doer. The blows he himself deals upon this spiritual faculty cut one of man's most certain bridges to the Infinite.

A powerful instrument, however, is his, if he choose to exert it. Some can hardly hear sense of right and wrong mentioned without confusing it with *the Will*, an intrinsic faculty

MAN, THE RULER

we should recognize apart from the use to which we put it. Helplessly set under the direction of man's conscious thought, it goes to deeper places, fetches far-reaching results, not only in outward manifestation, but primarily in himself. As the brain dictates *I will*, the owner is conscious of striking bedrock deep within, of developing his primeval, eternal self, of giving it such conscious direction and onward push that something far within him catches on to his intention and will continue to do his bidding even when his attention is otherwise occupied.

A pleasing sensation is experienced in wielding this inner power; probably at its height when directed upon something man desires to be altered, controlled, or adjusted in himself. It is here he can taste to the full the fruits of victory, forging for his future life an almost irresistible weapon, if he can but grasp that the will within him must conform to that Will of which it forms an infinitesimal echo—the Heaven Will, sustaining the universe.

Yet another set of sensations, spreading into a wide field, remains to be examined: sensations of the body.

Man's position is further complicated by insistent calls from the flesh. Hunger and thirst drive him hourly to action and may raise a combative creature within him. Pain, discomfort, fatigue, may swallow all other capabilities.

Sense the body as a thing apart; nourish, comfort, above all control it. Through power of mind be a wise father to it.

Weaknesses of the body, undetected and neglected, are allowed to flit across and entangle with qualities. Many a patient, hard-working mother allows fatigue to influence her temper to the detriment of happiness, preventing the reaping of just appreciation of her labour. Did she allow herself and others to recognize fatigue, this confusion might not occur. Again, the first weakening of will may be connected with thirst; though if thirst should happily lead to the strengthening of will, confusion is less likely to arise. The happy possessor of that will is fully aware of the force he employs.

Sensations of the body should be diagnosed, ministered to, checked, or ruled out by the direction of mind.

Existence is yet further complicated by perpetual notifications, swift, telegraphic in character, interrupting, speaking from the without at every moment of life, increasing pressure upon the human brain. Messages perpetually pour from the senses. The eyes see, ears hear, fingers touch. The conscious mind of man must sort, arrange, gather, remember from this bewildering kaleidoscope. These faculties are servants that never cease to serve us. We, in turn, should use them wisely, kindly.

In all things man is conscious of power within, stronger than anything that can be brought to bear from the outward. Some birthright, whereby we possess; some inner being that possesses is the king, hidden within the breast. Winds may blow, waves may beat—can we but enter within, we meet One who remains steadfast.

CHAPTER VI.

MAN IN TRINITY.

The Bible sprang from the Inner Doctrine chiefly in the form of stories, so that the unseeing eye and the unhearing ear are yet charmed and instructed with the outward thing they do not fully understand, much as pictures in a book may delight an unlettered man, who cannot read the writing.

Thus when God said to Abraham, *Get thee out of thy country, and from thy kindred, and from thy father's house,* the signification is that man must break with his body, with his senses, and his belief in his limited consciousness; for the body is the earth or bit of country we inhabit, the senses—each related to other and to us—represent the family, while our consciousness of mind makes us limit, as to a house, That Which is without limit, the All Father.[1]

Out of this smallness man must travel to

---

[1] See A. Franck on *The Kabbala.*

MAN IN TRINITY

inhabit a greater country, as yet unknown to him, where he will find both with him and in him the true Presence of the Unnameable blessing him ; and returning later to his home, perceive and adjust all in its true proportions, to appreciate and enjoy.

In the strange, moving story of Isaac in his blind old age, deceived by his younger son, Jacob, forced to deny the blessing to his first-born Esau, we discover Spirit, mind, and body —man's three concomitant parts, recognizable by himself—in the form of parable.

The Father, Spirit, strives to bless and find full expression in his earth-born son ; but conscious mind has come. His message cannot pass except by using mind as the channel to the body.

Esau, the earth-man, represents the body.

In strange corroboration of the tentative theory that man was first evolved unthinking as the beasts, he is called the first-born.

Jacob, conscious mind, is the younger brother. Though later evolved, not even the Father, Isaac, can now ignore nor pass over him. Mind in man usurps the place once given to instinct. He must come between Isaac and his elder earth-brother Esau. Spirit eternally remains the First, Mind the Second, passing the message to matter (or body), the Third.

Jacob, conscious mind, is told (let us not miss the point), because he is dwelling in the earth that the Lord of Life loves : *See, the smell of my son is the smell of a field which the Lord hath blessed : therefore God give thee of the dew of heaven and the fatness of the earth and plenty of corn and wine.*

Let people serve thee, and nations bow down to thee. Be lord over thy brethren and let thy mother's sons bow down to thee.

Mind must rule.

Yet if this is to be the lot of Jacob, Esau, the earth in man, cries to the Lord of Life : *Bless me, even me also, O my father !*

And Isaac his father answered and said unto him :

Behold, thy dwelling shall be in the fatness of the earth and of the dew of heaven from above.

And by thy sword shalt thou live, and shalt serve thy brother.

Once more the tussle of earth-existence is put plainly before man, with the added fact that, in this tussle, body must serve mind.

This mind thus depicted in Jacob is that limited consciousness we have seen Adam attain. The first feeble movement of Spirit in invisibility within the earth-crust of man, pushing through in such fashion that he may—if stupidly—be aware of Its Presence.

Again, foreshadowing follows of the yet higher Tree of Life, branching into such consciousness that man's incessant labour in his limited mind is to be lessened, if not ended. Esau is further told:

And it shall come to pass that when thou shalt have dominion, that thou shalt break his yoke from off thy neck.

When matter awakens to the presence of Spirit in its midst, man's mind will open to wider consciousness. Of the three parts, blending in one, neither will assert dominion over other, but all dwell in peace together.

Once more *the subtlety* of the conscious mind in man is demonstrated in this story of Jacob and once again associated with Woman.

Why should we find this conscious mind so closely knit with Woman ? Can it be that but for her influence, her forthgoingness, together with relationship with her, the responsibility that love and fatherhood lay upon man, he would be content to remain inert in mind ? Dumb in intellect ? Earth-bound ? Instinctive as beasts of the field ?

Again, we find Woman urging forward this push of consciousness in man.[1]

Once more this push is unpleasantly associated with slyness, the creep of the Serpent, and yet again plainly works against or postpones the straight blessing—the conscious habitation of Spirit in matter.

Again we are brought against the fact that the second urge of Spirit sensed consciously by man can have its evil as well as its good side.

Constant choice of his own action is now man's portion by virtue of this faculty.

Matter needs matter; the tempter, Jacob (conscious mind), prompts Esau (the body).

And he sold his birthright for a mess of pottage, as millions of thinking men for the same reason are doing at this moment. Jacob did not put plainly before him the choice of identifying himself with earth-material, or of rising above its chains to claim his just relationship with an Infinite Father.

Spirit, now cut from direct contact through blind instinct to man, can reach to the central

[1] An element of the Eternal Feminine in conscious mind (the continuation of that push to consciousness, first inaugurated by splitting humanity into two sexes) is expressed in Greek mythology by Athene, who sprang fully armed from the head of Jupiter.

spot of man's activity only by the bridge of man's conscious mind. Esau, for whom his father yearns, forfeits his place as firstborn through the advent of his brother Jacob; not only in the old Bible story, but here and now in each of us.

As though to reveal long years of slow evolution of man, the tale earlier tells that *Isaac entreated the Lord for his wife, because she was barren. And twins struggled within her.* Not without struggle, not without the constant urge of the Push from Spirit, the Second Power, the Verb—though yet dormant and totally unawakened in man's consciousness—was man evolved. An order of existence that repeats in every baby. First appears the body, next the mind. All work together for his consummation. Hard on the heel of the earth-man pushes the thought-man. *Two manner of people shall be separated from thy bowels; and the one people shall be stronger than the other people, and the elder shall serve the younger.*

Body must serve mind. Without the conscious direction of mind we cannot lift finger to mouth to give the body sustenance. And a certain enmity exists between them. Body or mind, one must go down before the will of the other. Nor is this tussle once and for ever. Again and again it arises. All through life, body and mind only know peace in faithfully and kindly serving each other.

Of the two, mind is compelled to take the leading part.

Yet beware of the mind that would either overwork the body (St. Francis calls it Brother Ass. *The merciful man is merciful to his beast*), or would bully it with anxiety, worry, and nervous fear. The mind that will perpetually dwell in the weak earth-side of Esau instead of abiding with strength and confidence in the Eternal Bosom of the Lord of Life. Both are children of One Heavenly Father. We must not let the Jacob within us debar Esau unduly from his rightful inheritance, any more than we must let Esau, the earth-man, dictate gross desire to Jacob, the conscious mind.

Danger lies, while reading the inner meaning of the parable, in identifying ourselves more closely with one of the three than with the others. This is man's initial mistake.

In our proper persons we are Isaac, Jacob, and Esau; Spirit, mind, and body. Not that we possess the full possibility of power of any one of the three, still, such as man is able to realize in himself—not one, but three. Not three, but one. *One altogether, not by confusion of the Substance, but by the Unity of the Person.*

The story presents a singularly perfect picture of the modifications necessarily set on the three elements, when striving to find expression in man before pure existence is attained. So that in ourselves at this instant we are the blind old Father, groping through love to his child; we are Esau, the first-born, reaching for red pottage; and Jacob, mind made conscious, scheming in the first place for his own advantage.

But in this narrow spot of self Jacob is not suffered to stay. As in the tale of Adam, the moment man's mind is lit with consciousness he is driven forth. His mother (the womb that conceives conscious thought, again an undying element in our essential selves) instantly perceives his precarious position. She drives him forth to the action that alone can preserve him.

Yet her love, eternally piercing him, is ever present in his being. Of Parent God, the Mother-Eternal turns to the Everlasting Father, crying over her son with lament and anguish: *I am weary of my life because of the daughters of Heth. If Jacob take a wife, such as these. . . .* Mother-yearn with Father-love for ever penetrates the earth-man with mind made conscious. Intense longing for good is irrevocably interwoven in the very fibre of being with capacity for evil.

Thus Spirit sends forth not merely His only-begotten Son, the Second Power in ray and movement, but the only-begotten Son in each one of us. Man illuminated by the ray of conscious mind; driven to independent use of it.

What use is he to make?

And the first night out from home (the place of belief in his body, his senses, and his conscious mind), *Jacob tarried, because the sun was set, took stones* (symbol of earth's crustaceous inertia), *and put them for his pillow.*

And he dreamed, and behold a ladder set up on earth, and the top of it reached to heaven.

Such is the conscious mind. Ladder between earth and heaven, up which—at man's bidding—angels or serpents ascend or descend.

Ladder betwixt the Lord of Life and the earth He loves.

Does man make of it a barrier? The way of the lying snake, the evil power? Or a passage?

And if a passage, a passing to and fro of angelic forces, then is he drawn to the Bosom of the Father, the actual Almighty Essence we—if we can only find ourselves—shall also find ourselves to be, and is himself the Verb, the Word, the daily Presence of Indwelling Spirit, becoming visible in the earth-body of man.

CHAPTER VII.

DISEASES OF THE SPIRIT.

CLEAR shining of the Spirit may be hidden, veiled, clouded from sight of its owners.

Where do the eyes go? Within to the hidden everlasting Glory? Without to a world of rapidly disintegrating atoms?

This within and without exist in all things. We cannot glimpse it in ourselves unless we perceive it in others. Every object on which we look has its everlasting Glory, and its rapidly disintegrating atoms. Which do we see?

And if *without*, to the passing show, to the miasma of illusion, to the quick fantasy of decay, has not man that within his own body, fatally attracting and drawing him to the false combination? Recombining him to elements of the dust to which some part of him already belongs?

This, then, is his *is*. By and through this portion of his existence he creates his *I am*, and is disappointed, disgusted, resentful at its disintegrating conditions. Fast, fast the vibrations fling, one corpuscle arises to die from another, binding conditions of birth just as the parent-man flings his health or disease, his desires and torments into the body of his son. Cell upon cell, the human frame is reborn hourly; conditions slowly altering along the chain of life, dominated by the uses put upon them. The body we walk in to-day is father to the one we shall be wearing a year hence, and ancestor to the one in which we shall walk in ten years' time.

Tastes, habits, desires not only can be, but ARE dictated to-day by the forefathers in our own bodies to cells and corpuscles yet to be born. Thus the *I am* never ceases to command the *I shall be*.

While I am young let me taste the glories of the flesh. And build the very essence of decaying death of the flesh into the tissues, nucleus, corpuscles of existence.

Instinctively we shield the child even from knowledge of gross, carnal wrong. Voices cry from far within that the beauty of his boyhood would be checked, destroyed. Every tiny cell within him would feel the wrong and send the shock through to far descendants. Flesh, thickened to gross desire, yearns to flesh,—ceases to feel the presence of Spirit.

Veils descend on the consciousness, befogging man. Fear, jealousy, greed—offspring of the lying serpent, creeping into human mind—must be seized and slain.

The first necessity is to detect these diseases in ourselves. No easy matter. Jealousy in particular oozes a blinding quality, like a thick veil, lying glibly to its owner. Happy the man or woman who can pick jealousy from their midst, pierce it as with a skewer and hold it for themselves to look upon.

Of these three, fear, jealousy, greed, no crime, no abasement of the human self is ever totally free. Chains that bind humanity, not from the without, but from the within.

Chains that hold the fatal combining power of inward attraction to their own like.

Gravitation is not stronger than attraction. Doubtless is—attraction. Like to like. Atmosphere to atmosphere.

Five veils hold Brahma from mortal ken.
1. *The veil of lustful Desire.*
2. *The veil of Malice.*
3. *The veil of Sloth and Idleness.*
4. *The veil of Pride and Self-righteousness.*
5. *The veil of Doubt.*

DISEASES OF THE SPIRIT

Are these the children of glad, free, immortal Spirit? Whence come they? Parasites of the flesh, dragging their owners through mire and mist of the everlastingly decaying, whining that it alone is real, and that our deathless life, our immortal love, and boundless intelligence are bound up in the appearance of the moment.

Where do the eyes go? Within to the everlasting Glory? Or without to a world of rapidly disintegrating atoms?

Are we to spend our lives like boys after butterflies, chasing the elusive? Or seeing its outward beauty as the symbol, the illusion of an everlasting eternal Force? Loving, pitying all men and things with the sense that One Father and one Mother, a thread uniting beads, is the essential essence of all? Bird, bee, and butterfly as well as ourselves. Are we to look on nothing but the outer appearance, the body of our beloved? If there is communion, where should it start, if not here, where mind is manifesting in flesh under the quickening of Immortal Spirit?

And in simply tasting this profound yet simple knowledge, miasmic clouds will lift, veils rend, and consciousness grow clear as we experience the deathlessness of each other,

Unless the Trinity contains its true proportions, unless the great elements co-relate and co-exist, man is falling from his balance.

Utter negation and neglect of the body will lead to its uselessness, if not its immediate death. Utter negation and neglect of the Spirit will lead to its uselessness, if not its immediate death.

Mind we thus see in its true proportion or element: the bridge, the channel from one to other, the life-leader, the way-shower, the mediator and advocate, the judge, who at some moments in all men's lives will crucify matter to Spirit or Spirit to matter. And if we too relentlessly sacrifice one part, the other, useless without it, must wane and perish. If we, by neglect, are hastening disintegration of one part, its withdrawal is enough to stifle the other portion of existence. Back to the scrap-heap!

Not only do solitary men return thus to the dissolution of their component parts; but we see this happening to civilizations of whole races of humanity.

Man, born to be higher than the angels, to be the living Verb and Word of immortal Spirit, loses his way, blindfolded in the forests of miasma, mists, and delusions. Greed and sloth sap his divine strength.

The Push-Power of Immortal Thought lifts him, through himself, through his own aims, exertions, ambitions, calculations into fairer, higher worlds in this one. He learns the use and control of material conditions, forcing them by brain and will to be his servants. Steam, electricity, combined effort go beneath his dominating power. Cities rise. Civilizations climb. Egypt, Peru, Persia, Rome.

Ichabod!

How did the Glory depart?

Disintegrating vibration was loosened by the inability to realize Indwelling Spirit and obey the happy Law of Life.

Civilization can never be reared to stay until all component parts of humanity find balance and equally aid and diffuse its benefits.

How is this to be done? By the heightening of each individual. Greed, selfishness, laziness, vice in one holds back the entire race. Like mountaineers upon a rope, all must climb together.

These diseases are catching. They are hopelessly infectious. The entire race must be rid of them by the conscious effort of each individual. Not one putting too much strain on the other; but each bearing burden for the sake of the rest.

One of the earliest dangers of civilization lies in its robbing man of his individual responsibility. One clings too much to the other. High intellects are produced; these are specialists; but even they are leaning for the necessities of existence upon others. Not alone and naked do any combat the conditions of life. It is easier to rely on the specializing efforts of the few than attain in oneself. Easy enough to step on a train about whose propulsion we know nothing. Easy enough to grumble at food, brought from far ends of the earth by the toil and sweat of men, on whose faces we never look. To buy lives and virtue of others. To put an ever-accumulating value upon coin. Easy enough to lose the real balance and health of existence, whose underlying Law says to all: If you think—consider. If you eat, sleep, wake—work: If you breathe —love.

Where are the little unloved children of the earth? Can such exist?

If so, beware of vaunted civilization.

Intelligent savages would know better how

to support life on a desert island than denizens of a prosperous city; though these may have travelled in trains, steamers, and aeroplanes, posted letters to far parts of the earth, and spoken there by telephone.

Yet it is not this leaning each on other that disintegrates civilization. Something more active, more false to man's own nature is necessary to pull it apart than the sharing of tasks, which may, in its essential action (as shown by ant and bee), be the correct leading of multiplicity towards unity.

What is at this moment destroying, killing, disintegrating our own civilization?

No man exists who cannot answer the question.

Let him look within and answer fairly to himself.

On the other hand, what power within him is actively building up civilization, so that each member, relying upon the assistance and dependability of the others, feels that not to himself alone, but to all humanity his every effort, his daily work, blesses and increases happiness?

This is the true civilization. The one that must last. This will bring man on through his own endeavour, through the mighty Urge within to the place where, almost unconsciously climbing the Tree of Knowledge, he will find its upper branches no less than the Tree of Life.

CHAPTER VIII.

HIDDEN MIND.

DEEP beneath our consciousness works an unending, industrious, wise mind.

Can the leopard change his spots? Most assuredly not by any will or conscious direction of his own. Yet science now answers that, however oblivious he may be of such a change, the spots or marking of his beautiful fur would present a miserable appearance did that fur not perish and renew with the same regularity as the human finger nails.

The tiniest molecule is as surely alive as the elephant, is existing by perpetual change, necessitating constant decay as well as growth; for intersecting, interwoven with decay is an eternal condition of life. Change, not death, is the abiding law of the universe.

And in this incessant change, in the undeviating common-sense, ruling with necessary direction every manifestation, even of parasitic life, we must recognize control by that

Moving Power for which we know no better name than Intelligence or Mind.

Though we are not aware of any thinking process that alters our digestive faculties, enabling them to follow vagaries we may be putting upon them, and though we cannot put ourselves in touch with an intelligence directing the construction of blood for the heart, yet such intelligence is there or our manifold divergencies could not be met.

Can we, then, in our own selves contemplate the Maker as Manifestation so far apart from the matter of which we are composed that this matter is simply running its course, as a top may be set spinning by some anterior projection?

On the other hand, does it fill us with dismay to know another Mind at work within every particle of the body? We can trust it to be more faithful, of greater common-sense than our own. Should we be inclined to resent, we need but watch the working of the Hidden Mind in insect, bird, and animal. *Go ask of the beasts, they shall teach thee.*

If, then, we are at the same time both unconscious instruments, yet in a sense possessors of a mind working in our midst, is it possible to become sufficiently aware of its presence to benefit consciously by its wise counsel ? Can we bring our brains into touch with this inward instruction ? Can some subtle sympathy of hidden force, as yet unknown to us, compel us to correct action and direct us by the sublime common-sense of the Mind that is in all ?

Possibly creative artists are amongst those in closest conscious touch with Hidden Mind. Poets, writers, painters, musicians, sculptors, architects, actors; all who from apparent void draw images of beauty. An uprush of feeling, rather than of thought, first heats them, drives, and compels them to find expression.

They live on the confines of a wider world, that they may open portals to others on magic scenes, more real possibly to them than the objects with which they find themselves actually surrounded.

These men and women literally leave father, mother, wife, and child to climb into realms of whose presence they can only hope to make others aware by bringing them—sometimes in clumsy baskets—fragments, sweet as flowers, that they have gleaned in their wanderings. They are obliged to find body for these children of their own imagination, which mind evolves, sometimes painfully, though, again, some gem may be flung into their conscious midst so that it is suddenly there, a living thing, a harmony, without the painful travail of heaping thought upon thought. Some subtle sympathy of hidden force compels the possessor to correct action. Cosmic intelligence touches, enlightens their own. Flame is caught from other flame; flame of the Living Spirit, moving into matter by mind.

The engineer, the chemist, the inventor, all who by industrious effort acquire knowledge within the self, know those leaping moments of enlightenment, when from orderly arrangement of knowledge gained, the personal thought constructs, builds, projects; possibly into places as yet unknown.

Less commonly known to higher civilization are other manifestations of Universal Mind, though working unconsciously within a man, yet lighting his brain.

Queer affinities, occult sympathies between men and beasts off the track of deafening cities; the knowledge that works simultaneously into consciousness of shepherd and dog; the bodily suffering of the African tiger-man at the mutilation of a tiger; the obedience of poisonous serpents to the thin, piping whistle of the juggler, who knows from his within to their within how to entangle them in some strange mesmerism.

These things—uncanny to the town-inhabitant, who has closed these connexions with the All-mind in cultivation of his local one—are simple and natural as the act of breath to those whose consciousness is in frequent and yet, strange paradox, unconscious touch with the mind that is in all. Of such is the intuitive knowledge shown in the phenomenon of telepathy,[1] occasionally experienced among the natives of India and those of Central Africa. They know. They know events that can only reach the intelligence of their white officers by telegram or special message. They do not know how they know. They do not have to make special arrangements to know. It is known. Far within the man, hidden from his conscious, calculating thought, some spring can yield to the touch of Universal Intelligence, receive the news and impart it, without confiding to him the manner in which it is done.

Of such also is the power of clairvoyance, pre-vision, clairaudience. Whether working

[1] This telepathy was sometimes known in the forecastle of the British Navy before the coming of wireless telegraphy.

forward into the future to foretell coming events or groping back to the past to learn lost historical occurrences, or exercising that strange gift of seeing that which is now occurring at long distances, some slit is made in the dense veil of unconsciousness. The thing as it is slips through into the place in man's brain that knows. If there is uncertainty, it is because the veil or mist of man's thinking limitation closes about it. The thing is. Man's consciousness is capable of realizing the fact.

One point is certain: these things are not known from the without to the within; but deep from the within they climb to the without.

It is possible that certain knowledge is not usually passed into the ordinary, thinking brain of man. On the other hand, it is highly probable that certain filterings may first stay with us as survivals of those days when the All-Mind, working through man, was hidden from his consciousness, and that yet other filterings will again reach us as we approach higher states of consciousness.

It is not by crude denial, but by gentle perseverance and scientific study of phenomena that ignorance in ourselves can be finally guided to true understanding.

What we do not understand is doubtless understood and caused by the Mind that knows and accomplishes all, though we are quite capable of putting false interpretations upon it.

Hasty conclusions, dangerous as denials, should be carefully avoided. Let us not greedily seize, but stand patiently by and watch with suspicious eyes—not so much the unexpected, as our own limitations.

Have we a memory, deeper, far more consecutive and truthful than the cupboard we habitually store and use? How is it on revisiting a place, smelling a scent, hearing a forgotten name, memories swarm back upon us, a moment before completely lost to conscious recollection?

Is all really stored safely within us? Waiting to be reawakened? Waiting to be weighed and judged by our own larger conceptions of wider life?

Sweet, entrancing experience suddenly to recall the pure, generous impulse of some childish act. To taste again a loving-kindness, long since forgotten, blindly accepted at the time. Seeing it now with ripened view, appreciating its true quality.

Could hell of flames have worse agony to offer than our own blind, idiotic actions, returning upon our memory with the full force of their far-reaching results? Happily the interblend of life will give relief from such memories by others that sweeten and relieve.

Is it possible that this veil upon recollection may split and rend and let all in upon the consciousness as the Temple of the Body (as we now know it) gives place to something different?

Will Mind, the Second Power in ourselves, return in full recollection upon us? Will it *come again in power to judge both the quick and the dead?*

Is matter or mind or Spirit creating this merciful veil that we be not overloaded? Here we doubtless touch the intimate, interblending of all three, co-existing, co-relating, possibly co-eternal.

The balance of brain depends upon bodily conditions; yet, being balanced, is useless unless it be fed by mind to use powers of Spirit. We are lost in a maze of bewilderment unless we hold firmly to the healthy intermingling of all three parts. This, however, is not to say that the particular matter our eyes can now see is the end and finish of all matter. It is as ignorant to say a thing does not exist because the immediate lens granted to our bodily vision is not focussed to it, and therefore does not perceive it, as to say a thing does exist because these our eyes happen to be able to focus it to just such an appearance.

Infinite variety and possibility surround and uphold us. Not yet do we even know what we are, how then can we hope to sense what we may be? Eyes have not seen, nor these human ears heard.

CHAPTER IX.

THE KINGDOM OF MATTER.

MAN's initial mistake lies in his contempt of matter. At heart he despises the stuff of which he is made. If he reverenced it, he would slay the beast in himself and strangle the power of the snake.

In the beginning the Bible tells us that *God made man out of the dust of the earth, and breathed into him the breath of life.* It closes by saying, *The Spirit and the Bride say, Come.* Dust of the earth, consciously inhabited by Spirit, is raised to the Heavenly Bride. We should construe, Dust of the earth = Bride. Breath of Life = Spirit. In all things lifting the vessel chosen to its appointed position.

We break down our own bridge from Infinite Goodness to matter by despising, treating with contempt the body. If we felt awe, reverence, and an uplifted sense of being capable stewards for the just appreciation and use of every cell and molecule within it, we should never dare put it to vile or mean use.

If we trusted matter to be endowed with intrinsic health and strength, greedy grasping must drop away, as would stupid sloth and dull inertia. *Consider the lilies of the field.* Many a man is more capable of reverencing and respecting a flower than he does his own flesh; while many of us think it will be better cared for than we. And why?

Because we have been given power, are endowed with freedom, conscious thought, and action to fetch for ourselves the sustenance of which we stand in need. Why are we anxious? Because some are too lazy to secure nourishment, and others in greed would overreach and deprive a neighbour. This race-injustice has a stultifying effect upon us. Not that men are likely to put forth equal effort, strength, courage; but he that is stronger should be mindful of the weaker, while sloth, idleness, lack of caution and forethought, or vice must reap the reward of decay. Only those gifted with the use of independent mind thus transgress from the primary Law of Being—Spirit's first movement in Divine Energy. It is this transgressing that is man's undoing.

The source of evil lies in man's misuse of his

limited mind. With the attaining of consciousness, we start an anxious, selfish, independent action of the human mind, alienating us from the Cosmic Intelligence, the Heaven Will, Whose behest is obeyed by all sane life in the universe. This alienation from the Great Spirit, Whose first movement is Cosmic Intelligence, brings about disintegration of the three component parts, balancing us into existence, body, mind, and Spirit. First paralysis sets in, with a disability to sense our constituents. If the three parts sunder, literal death occurs of the human entity established by them; while the three elements, Spirit, mind, and body, losing that particular connexion, slip back separately to original essence to be utilized in fresh combination. In other words, individual identity is lost.

Thus the selfish or slothful use of the mind we gained with Adam may be literal barrier or death to the urge of Spirit, trying to manifest consciously in the flesh.

The sense of self which Spirit engenders as the first step to consciousness is apt to assume undue proportions in its possessor, to take on anxiety or greed with personal responsibility; while if it lack sufficient fire to add this sense of personal responsibility, the instinctive urge to industry being withdrawn, the man falls into sloth, and subsequently starvation.

Happily for us, Spirit is so powerful that but a little opening of gates to its Presence in industry, loving action, generous deeds, in all good and healthy impulse, floods our being (even if unconsciously) with renewal of forces and sets freely flowing the three-fold interaction of Life Eternal.

Matter has long been regarded with a contempt it does not deserve. It is *potentiality*; how are we *actualizing* it?

We are doing it by the constructive power of thought-force; and if we would discover humanity's arch hypocrite and snake, it is precisely to this thought-force, this mind in man we must look.

No action of man's is potentialized without the concurrence of his conscious thought. Character, governing action, is developed or retarded by it. Acts bear fruit, not only in the visible result of the moment, but into our invisible selves, into our children and grandchildren, to become the building-structure of the human race.

Behind each act, however small or trifling, thought commands; angel or demon in himself no man can elude. Conscious mind, whether it will or not, must be the keeper of his brother, body.

To prevent disaster we must get personally into the ark of safety. We must find within ourselves the Noah—*a just man and perfect in his generation*; we must *walk awhile with God*. We must float over the waters of illusion, taking with us into the Ark the essential things that matter in our lives,[1] so that they germinate and bring forth fresh activities; while the corrupt, the reptile, and the swine perish in the flood.

Let the rainbow remain ever the symbol, the sign set in Heaven, that the earth quality in man is blessed; that the First Power of the Trinity penetrates, finds expression in the Third.

I do set my bow in the cloud, and it shall be for a token of a covenant between me and the earth.

Earth is no more to be cursed; for mind, not body, is the culprit. *And the Lord said, I will not again curse the ground any more for man's sake.* And why not? Because the fault lies elsewhere. *For the imagination of man's heart is evil from his youth.* In spite of

[1] Let a man ask himself, What matters to me most in life? Let him search within and find the reply.

THE KINGDOM OF MATTER

obstructions, earth is again to be filled with His Presence and blessed. *That I may remember the Everlasting Covenant between God and every living creature of all flesh that is upon the earth.*

Reverence for the earth, that actually is the Lord's in the sense that He inhabits, vivifies, and possesses it, should enter into our daily association with all around us, lifting the common cup of life into sacrament. Such mighty creative power lies in our own imagination that things actually are to us solely as we regard them. The highest allegory, unfolding before our eyes humanity's noblest task, is that of mother and child. Spirit eternally reverences the Virgin-womb of matter, raising it in creation to the Mary Mother.

And the earth was of one language and one speech. Men understood each other before they used speech to darken understanding and thought to alienate sympathy.

Differing languages are but a reflection of the condition of mind within, like all strong inward conditions, thrown into outward appearance, not to confuse, but to shield nations by their veils of non-comprehension from yet more bitter misunderstanding.

It is a light thing not to know each other's speech; a cruel, snake-like thing to suspect and distrust each other's thought.

Always this babel of confusion and distrust is reared upon pride. Pride in ourselves, our own habits and manners, measuring and condemning other men and nations by the narrow conditions we ourselves may have experienced. Mind again, not body, is the culprit. Lucifer has fallen. Mind, the channel of light, is darkened. Unable to remain inert, it must work good or it will work evil.

If we would know and apply the hidden meaning in the history of the children of Israel, of the Egyptians and of Pharaoh, we must seek for these people in ourselves. Nor can we realize Moses until we meet him face to face in the interior of our own consciousness. Is the wise and mighty Law-giver reigning there, or the greedy, avaricious, self-seeking Pharaoh? Do we rule our thoughts, or are they troubled as tribes, driven hither and thither by the lash of a tyrant?

Do we see God, good, in all we meet? Or do we sense fear, injustice, tribulation? Either in Egypt or the Promised Land we must dwell, not in the without, but the quiet within of our own breasts.

THE KINGDOM OF MATTER 93

Not by glossing over, but by sheer vigorous fight, even as Jacob wrestled the night long, must we prevail. Man has far to go, has heights to climb. Not by dallying on sunny slopes of petted self, but by forcing enemies within him beneath his feet, shall he rise as upon a footstool to his appointed place, the right hand of God.

And which way does he prefer? What does his nature crave? We are equipped for glorious battle. Not until we achieve can we even desire to enter into rest.

No man can grasp a revelation unless he be ready for it. Moses grasped the inner hidden meaning of the illuminating revelation on which is built the structure not only of the Bible, but of all creation, and the very Temple of God—His habitation to be made visible—man. He heard the Hidden Name, the Name of Power; in its strength went forth, became Statesman, General, and finally conquered.

Now Moses inquired of the Lord. He wrestled with his own consciousness until he gained the knowledge for which he yearned. *When I come to the children of Israel and say unto them, The God of your fathers hath sent me unto you, and they shall say unto me, What is his name? What shall I say unto them?*

Into the void he threw the question. Certainly in anguish, possibly in doubt.

And God said unto Moses:

I AM THAT I AM.

Intersecting, penetrating Power passes into all things. Nothing in creation can be left out. Every single object on which the eye falls is as that Mysterious Bush, flaming with Living Spirit, burning with inward, moving fire, yet not consumed. God, like fire, cannot cease from action. Every hair of our heads is not only numbered, but also sustained, is alive by the eternal Power and Presence of the Living God.

This sense of the Presence of Indwelling Spirit in all things poured in upon Moses. In the light of this revelation he perceived the Promised Land, though unable to penetrate. He saw it from afar off. One was to come, the latchet of whose shoe not he, nor yet any of us, was worthy to unloose, Who was in His Own Person the great I AM. He was not only to see, but to BE THAT of which God spake.

Yet Moses cleared the ground for all men. He erected the first great signposts to lead men from the tangled wilderness of their conscious minds towards the Promised Land, where men in full and happy consciousness shall regain the connexion, temporarily lost, with the Hidden Mind sustaining all. These signposts are headed—*Thou shalt not*. This is the first struggle we must make; ruling out of existence deterrent, downward tendencies, learning to sense the source of evil as lying in the misuse of man's limited mind, determinedly controlling it; holding fast to the plain *Thou shalt not*, speaking its sane, inward command, and so through steadfast obedience climbing to larger, wider places; though we may have to overcome, as with the very sharpness of death itself, before we open within to the Kingdom of Heaven.

We may stand, uncovered, in reverence and understanding, as Moses did before that desert bush, before everything that is made, however great, however small, and know it to be by the invisible Glory of God—good. And we may go forth with fresh power in this knowledge to confront and disable the false in us, lead our bewildered selves out of the mazes, and gain at last the Land, promised to us by every aspiration and desire of our hearts, finding as an actual fact that if Supreme Being is thus sensed, met, and conjoined with matter, the mind of man slips automatically into correct place, joins the Second Power of the Trinity, and becomes the bridge from Infinite to finite.

If we could but simplify, when we say Supreme Being, instead of translating the word into Personality, regarding God truly as BEING, then instead of finite in all dilemmas screaming to Infinite, the clear, still voice of Infinite would be heard incessantly within, guiding, guarding, speaking to finite.

CHAPTER X.

MAN, THE VERB.

THE reverse of disintegration is power of attraction, the combining of energies, holding together, creating adhesion.

What principle of life in ourselves can we regard as the active force doing these things? Of creating adhesion? Attraction?

Work.

In no situation does man more fully sense and grasp his three constituents, body, mind, and Spirit, than when he is in his own person the living Verb.

I ought passes through his being with insistent call. From far infinite realms travels the small voice to tap persistently within the channel of his mind until his will has mastered the materials around him and passed action from the infinite into the plastic condition of finite matter; so that others as well as himself can turn and behold his act.

I can. Mountains may encompass the

pioneer, vast wastes beyond it, unknown, untrodden, people at his back who may not take the trouble to reap the fruit for which he bled and sweated. *I can* rings through his being and into his acts. Verb of the Living Spirit, by inward power he achieves.

I must. Strange propulsion from the depths of the within leaves no rest, day or night, until power is put forth, and, no leaf on breeze, but man at the quiet, calculating, dominating summit of manhood, travailing as mother with child, brings forth from the within power that will force events on the without.

I will. What is this *I*? Is it some little local self, made of interpolated scraps of earthly parents, things picked up at school, blood-vessels, corpuscles, and habits that utters this deep *I*, pitting that tiny person against multitudes? Using a hammer that may dash its small frame every time it is wielded? Deep from the recesses of that local self surge up, like a sea, unfathomed forces. In his own limited self man can be that mighty hammer of will, plied by the Everlasting Ego, the Almighty *I*, who stands, alone, at the back of everyone. Each man should find a name for this Limitlessness behind his actions. Each should find his own name. To one

God may say all; to another, almost nothing. Inherent Intelligence may shout a living message to one mentality, and sound like a species of blasphemy to a third. *I will give him a white stone: and in the stone a name is written that no man knoweth save he that hath it.*

I have. Strange power of grasp and holding. What have you? Love and respect of those around you? Admiration and laughter of little children? Tie of sympathy with fellow beings? Can you add these to all other possessions you may enumerate?[1] Then you have the Heavenly Inheritance and are indeed the Heir of that Power Whose rain falls on the just and the unjust.

I shall not. Shut the door on the false and untrue. Build a wall about your being. Only One on earth can pull it down. The One that reigns in your own breast.

I do. And in doing, fulfil being, entering into the very law of creation, which knows one persistent act, creation. Old leaves are falling. New buds are springing. Ants building. Men making. Let us catch on to the joy of

[1] *"These sons belong to me, and this wealth belongs to me, with such thoughts is a fool tormented. He himself doth not belong to himself, how much less sons and wealth."* (" *Dhammapada, or Path of Virtue,*" translated from Pali by Max Müller.)

existence and let the Mighty Creator, at this instant without our knowledge creating fresh cells in our bodies, pass through the very centre of conscious thought, enabling us to contemplate as victor the things we too have done.

Laws of this Inward Might adjust powers as helm a ship. Love, gentleness, tolerance, that sense of true balance often finding expression in humour, accompany the compelling acting power of the Passing Verb, so soon as we recognize our Source and Origin and set ourselves in willing accord to become its servant.

Then do the words of the great Way-shower spring to fresh meaning. Far beneath is left the petty, the small, the struggling. One needs company, help for a mile? Let us go with him two. If needful, ten! This puny one would smite the cheek? Strength upon strength swells up from within and the without assumes due proportions. And forgive? Yes, unto seventy times seven. Who can touch? Who can reach the Deathlessness within us?

Take the power of push into oneself, instead of being pushed. Power will generate in the system; the greater the difficulty, the higher one lifts on the Cross of Spirit into matter.

Be love; be the thing itself, not its chosen tool. Be the I Am instead of the *Thou art*.

The Creative Mind of all is impersonal, and in this growth the importance of the petty personality slips away. A commanding attitude taken in small things to-day gives dominion and mastery over bigger things on the morrow; because sluices have been opened to the Infinite Working Energy behind, below, above, through all. By the same law that a razor, slightly sharpened, put away will sharpen itself, inward activities set going in a man's nature, by virtue of the Hidden Mind that carries on the task, continue, ripen, while the man's conscious attention strays elsewhere.

Realizing man as the Verb we must remember there are not three Powers, but One Power, nor is there One Power, but three Powers. The Verb itself is not only the Second Movement, but is the Generated Element and the Substance of the Universe. Let man find himself in his proper person a microscopic part of the (1) Substance, (2) the Pure Mind, and (3) the Generated Element, and he touches all.

Man, the Verb, is covered in matter as with a cloak; for that which is compelled into his use for his present occasions is not strong enough to behold the light of his own interior glory. Let us identify ourselves, if only momentarily, with the Creating Power within, and even the dumb body, incapable of full comprehension, will rejoice and live more fully in every part. Even if a man cannot mentally grasp this condition of being within him, work, action, deeds, especially loving, generous deeds, will put him in inward connexion with Unseen Power.

There IS a Light, internally lighting every man that cometh into the world.

That Light is not a mere ray, an expression, the Power; but IS Divine Spirit, God, the Unnameable, the Glory.

CHAPTER XI.

THE CHRIST-CONSCIOUSNESS.

To him that overcometh will I give the Tree of Life which is in the midst of the Paradise of God.

It is as difficult for us to realize the Christ-consciousness as it would have been for men who had not acquired the Adam-consciousness to grasp Adam's knowledge of mind and understand the interior working of his intelligence.

To those living instinctively as the beasts, such dominion as Adam received with the quickening of the conscious mind would be beyond their imaging capacity. Before they could even imagine it, they must have possessed a power of mind still beyond their reach.

If before Adam the conscious mind of man, as we now know it, lay enfolded in sleep, unawakened, so are we lost in the mists and miasmas of dreams, compared with the quickened awakening still in store for us.[1]

[1] *Awake, thou that sleepest, and Christ shall give thee Light.*

104 THE LAW OF BEING

Can we even lift our conceptions to grasp fully the Mind That Is In All ? How, then, are we to begin to picture the Glory, everlastingly generating it, our Heavenly Father ?

Even language debars conception. His unique Form embraces all forms and sex. We commit irreverence when compelled in our limitation to speak of the Unnameable as either He, She, or It.

Looking around we believe we see all that is; yet nothing can be easier than for the Mind that is in all to vivify matter which these particular material eyes of ours are quite incapable of seeing. Indeed it would be absurd to suppose that Mind creating in ant and bee and man eyes that can see everything. We see our immediate environments, the things that belong to our present condition. We perceive the stuff for the moment vivified for our use.

If in perceiving it, we would glorify it, gates in our consciousness would open to wider places. If we paused even once a day and said within ourselves I AM THAT which vivifies this matter, identifying ourselves with the Eternal Force within, perhaps no alteration would be immediately perceptible, we might slide back the next instant to identifying our-

THE CHRIST-CONSCIOUSNESS

selves with the outward shell, yet some profound and subtle adjustment could not fail to take place. Depths within would be reinforced.

The Christ-consciousness enjoys dominion over Spirit and mind as confidently as we sense body, with this vital difference:—that we, dealing only with one part in three, are incapable of holding even that one in the just equilibrium that would be simple and natural were we in conscious intercourse also with the other two parts of being.

By the living force of BEING, while in the flesh, Jesus of Nazareth walked on the water, penetrated to the agony point of sufferers with such flow of Life that He healed, and, tasting the Glory of Invisible Spirit, reversed the disintegrating action of the Second Power, brought It to Its true task again, the vivifying of matter, to such degree that He could raise the dead. He entered into possession of the Second Power of the Trinity, unhindered by human obstruction. He tasted of the Tree of Life. He became as the gods.

If we would realize some reflection of the Power universally His, we need but look at the love He inspires in men far down and through the centuries and know the cry He uttered, *I in them and Thou in Me*, is literally answered by the oneness men feel for this Man of the World's Sorrow, acquainted with the grief of all. And why this love, this human, binding tie? Because there is within all One Divine Spot. Touch that Spot and we are One, even as the Father, in, through and above us, is One.

Most strange of all, He healed sin, not only when He walked the earth, but, as sufferers in this sad particular could tell, here and now. He alters desire (or the verb and movement) in the breasts of men.

We should thank the High Intelligence directing all things that such gigantic possibilities cannot be loosed in us until we are wise enough to put them to perfect use.

Conscious mind in man must first rise to its rightful place. So soon as the power of thought in man is directed into sane channels, Lucifer will be restored as Angel of Light. Lucifer must be restored. Yet strange is the paradox. Not until Lucifer is restored—not until the equilibrium is so perfectly balanced that the Light lighting every man that cometh into the world shines through, glorified by the lantern containing it—can Lucifer be restored. That is, nothing but the conscious effort of the individual, each raising his own self through renunciation, through endeavour, training his

THE CHRIST-CONSCIOUSNESS

mind, reverencing his body, realizing himself as Spirit—such effort alone can restore the equilibrium of the three parts, necessary to enable the mind to pour through man with Angel-power, the demon itself, transfigured, raised.

Then, but not till then, will Lucifer rise with wings, bringing light, instead of confusion, into man.

Brightest and Best of the Sons of the Morning, Lucifer will find his ancient place and, prevailing, bring again all that was lost; for, his seat regained with added power, nothing can be lost; all will be raised into the Path that led there.

Which path are we, individually, cutting?

It is the supreme experiment of all.

We might hold our breath and shudder in anticipation of failure were it not for the great ones who have achieved.

All good impulse, love, generosity, work, seem to be expanding in tendency. All weaker impulse narrows down, drives man against his own walls.

Sin is lack of balance, loss of equilibrium.

Sloth is the exaggeration of man's rest.

Greed devours the man who does not know where accumulation for self should cease.

THE LAW OF BEING

Pride is the over-toppling of the sensitive instinct of personal responsibility.

The same ingredients are in all men; the art of balancing them is wanting in some. Inside each man can be found Herod and Pontius Pilate, Nathaniel without guile, Judas, honest Peter, and John, who can lean into the very bosom of the Lord. Surely as these are within him, deep in his farthest centre lives the Child, waiting for his own words, own encouragement to increase in grace, wax strong in wisdom: for unto each of us this *Child is born, unto us this Son is given.* It is upon His shoulders we should lay the government and call *His Name Wonderful, Counsellor, the Mighty God, the Everlasting Father, the Prince of Peace:* until, growing in favour of God, man shall come to the measure of the stature of the fullness of Christ.

Jesus of Nazareth, who prevailed, would have all be as He is. Each man not the little he, but the great He. Each man, not the petty I, but THAT upon which our eyes can barely look, the I AM.

Could we bear the blaze of glory, we should see this Presence in all around us. We should find this Golden One in everyone we meet, and finding Him in others would be our true

THE CHRIST-CONSCIOUSNESS 109

selves, for the Christ goes down to the One that really is. Not only in fellow men, but in all things we should be aware of the Hidden Glory. We should know the Divine Presence saying: *I am Alpha and Omega, the beginning and the end, the first and the last.* Nothing is too small, too common to be left out. I AM—*the Alpha and Omega, the first and the last.*

All that we see or touch is the garment wherewith God clothes Himself to become visible to His outermost particles. No cup we drink, no food we eat, but is His blood poured out freely, His Body broken on the Tree of Knowledge and of Life.

He is in the world and the world is made by Him, but the world knows Him not.

He comes unto His own, and His own receive Him not.

But as many as receive Him, to them gives He power to become the Sons of God, even to them that believe on His name.

Even in the Name of Power, I AM THAT I AM.

In the light of this truth, equilibrium restored, we find ourselves as in a Paradise of God. Tastes simplify, life grows calm, joys deepen.

God is still waiting to perfect Godhead in Manhood. To be perfect God in man, He must be perfect man; for, although man, *touching his godhead, is equal to the Father*, yet so long as he lingers in the Adam-consciousness must he remain inferior. For: *It is not by conversion of Godhead into flesh* (that is, not by remaining content in realizing his divine birth in the man he now is), *but by taking of that manhood into God, so although he be god and man, yet he is not two—but One, Christ.*

We must leave beneath us the old husk, man, burst from the sheath and soar through power into glory, the risen Christ.

For the earnest expectation of the creature waiteth for the Manifestation of the Sons of God.